GROWING

MW00914722

Jesus DID NOT call Peter Satan!

An examination of Matthew 16:21-23
using Ancient Bible Study methods

Michael Harvey Koplitz

All Scripture quotations, unless otherwise noted, are taken from the New American Standard Bible®, Copyright © 1960, 1962, 1963, 1968, 1971, 1972, 1973, 1975, 1977, 1995 by the Lockman Foundation. Used by permission. (www.Lockman.org)

The NASB uses italic to indicate words that have been added for clarification. Citations are shown with large capital letters.

Published by Michael H. Koplitz

ISBN: 9781711782478

Jesus DID NOT call Peter Satan!

Table of Contents

The main differences between the Greek method and the Hebraic method of teaching.....................................7

Methodology 13

Matthew 16:21-23...23

Works Cited...41

Jesus DID NOT call Peter Satan!

Introduction

The idea that Jesus called Peter Satan has never sat well with me. I learned this in the church and again in Seminary. The church and Seminary use the Greek/Western ways of learning and teaching. Unfortunately, the Scripture is not a Greek/Western document. Instead, it is a Semitic document. It needs to be read and treated that way. Unfortunately, when the church separated itself from its mother religion it also rejected the Semitic way of reading and understanding the Scripture. Therefore, misinterpretations and mistranslations were bound to occur.

By using Ancient Bible Study Methods, a student of the Scripture can discover what the original meaning of the Scripture is. It is a complicated process at first because the student has to abandon Greek/Western thinking. Once that is done, the original meaning of the Scripture will shine through.

This book examines Matthew 16:21-23 for its original meaning. The conclusion is that Jesus DID NOT call Peter Satan. Several articles are included about Ancient Bible Study Methods and the difference between the Greek and Hebraic methods of teaching.

As you discover the original meaning of the Scripture, you will find that you will want to learn more.

The main differences between the Greek method and the Hebraic method of teaching

Once a student becomes aware of these two teaching styles, the student will be able to determine if the class attended or if a book read, whether the teaching method is either a Greek or Hebraic method. In the Greek manner, the instructor is always right because of advanced knowledge. In the college situation, it is because the professor has his/her Ph.D. in some area of study, so one assumes that he or she knows everything about the topic. For example, Rodney Dangerfield played the role of a middle-aged man going to college. His English midterm was to write about Kurt Vonnegut Jr. Since he did not understand any of Vonnegut's books he hired Vonnegut himself to write the midterm. When he received the paper from the English Professor told Dangerfield that whoever wrote the paper knew nothing about Vonnegut. The professor's words are an example of the Greek method of teaching. Did the Ph.D. English professor think that she knew more about Vonnegut's writings than Vonnegut did? [1]

In the Greek teaching method, the professor or the instructor claims to be the authority. If one attends a Bible study class and the class leader says, "I will teach you the only way to understand this biblical book," you may want to consider the implications. This method is standard since most Seminaries and Bible colleges teach a Greek mode of learning, which is the same method the church has been utilizing for centuries.

---

[1] *Back to School*. Performed by Rodney Dangerfield. Hollywood: CA: Paper Clip Productions, 1986. DVD.

Hebraic teaching methods are different. The teacher wants the students to challenge what they hear. It is through questioning that a student can learn. Also, the teacher wants his/her students to excel to a point where the student becomes the teacher.

If two rabbis come together to discuss a passage of Scripture, the result will be at least ten different opinions. All points of view are acceptable if each is supported by biblical evidence. It is permissible and encouraged that students develop many ideas. There is a depth to God's Word, and God wants us to find all His messages contained in the Scripture.

Seeking out the meaning of the Scriptures beyond the literal meaning is essential to understand God's

Word fully.[2]   The Greek method of learning the Scriptures has prevailed over the centuries. One problem is that only the literal interpretation of Scripture was often viewed as valid, as prompted by Martin Luther's "sola literalis" meaning that just the literal translation of Scripture was accurate. The Fundamentalist movements of today base their beliefs on the literal interpretation of the Scripture. Therefore, they do not believe that God placed more profound, hidden, or secret meanings in the Word.

The students of the Scriptures who learn through Hebraic training and understanding have drawn a different conclusion. The Hebrew language itself leads to different possible interpretations because of

---

[2] Davis, Anne Kimball. *The Synoptic Gospels*. MP3. Albuquerque: NM: BibleInteract, 2012.

the construction of the language. The Hebraic method of Bible study opens avenues of thought about God's revelations in the Scripture never considered. Not all questions about the Scripture studied will have an immediate answer. If so, it becomes the responsibility of the learners to uncover the meaning. Also, remember that many opinions about the meaning of Scripture are also acceptable.

Jesus DID NOT call Peter Satan!

Methodology

The methodology employed is to use First Century Scripture study methods integrated with the customs and culture of Jesus's day to examine the Hebrew and Christian Scriptures, thus gathering a more in-depth understanding by learning the Scriptures in the way the people of Jesus's day did.

I have titled the methodology of analyzing a passage of Scripture in a Hebraic manner the "Process of Discovery." The author developed this methodology, which brings together various areas of linguistic and cultural understanding. There are several sections to the process, and not all the parts apply to every passage of Scripture. The overall result of developing this process is to give the reader a framework for studying the word in more depth.

The "Process of Discovery" starts with a Scripture passage. An examination of the linguistic structure of the passage is next. The linguistic structure includes parallelism, chiastic structures, and repetition. Formatting the passage in its linguistic form allows the reader to be able to visualize what the first century CE listener was hearing. Their corresponding sections label the chiasms, for example, A, B, C, B', A.' Not all passages of the Scriptures have a poetic form.

The next step is to "question the narrative." The questioning the narrative process assuming the reader knows nothing about the passage. Therefore, the questions go from the simple to the complex.

The next task is to identify any linguistic patterns. Linguistic patterns include, but are not limited to irony, simile, metaphor, symbolism, idioms, hyperbole, figurative language, personification, and allegory.

A review of any translation inconsistencies discovered between the English NAU version and either the Hebrew or Greek versions is done. There are times when a Hebrew or Greek word is translated in more than one way. Inconsistencies also can be created by the translation committee, which may have decided to use traditional language instead of the actual translation. The decision of the translation committee is in the Preface or Introduction to the Bible. Perhaps some of the inconsistencies were intentionally added to convey some deeper meaning. An examination for every discrepancy is done.

The passage is analyzed for any echoes of the Hebrew Scriptures in the Christian Scriptures. Using a passage from the Hebrew Scriptures in the Christian Scriptures, an echo occurs.[3] Also, echoes are found when Torah (Genesis through Deuteronomy) passages are used in other Hebrew Bible books. Cross-references in the Scripture are references from one verse to another verse which can assist the reader in understanding the verse.

The names of persons mentioned in the passage are listed. Many of the Hebrew names have meaning

---

[3] Mitzvot are the 613 commandments found in the Torah that please God. There are positive and negative commandments. The list was first development by Maimonides. The full list can be found at: ttp://www.jewfaq.org/613.htm.

and may be associated with places or actions. Jewish parents used to name their children based on what they felt God had in store for their child. An example of this is Abraham, whose original name was Abram and was changed to mean eternal father (God changed Abram's name to Abraham, indicating a function he was to perform). When the Hebrew Bible gives names, many of the occurrences mean something unique. The same importance can occur for the names of places. The time it takes to travel between locations can supply insight into the event.

Keyphrases are identified in verses when they are essential to an understanding of that passage. There are no rules for selecting the keywords. Searching for other occurrences of the keywords in Scripture in a concordance is necessary to understand the word's usage; this must be done in either Hebrew or Greek, not in English. A classic Hebraic approach is to find the usage of a word in the Scripture by finding other verses that contain the word. The usage of a word, in its original language, is discovered by searching the Scripture in the language of the word. Verses that contain the word are identified, and a pattern for the usage of the word discovered. Each verse is examined to see what the usage of the word is which, may reveal a model for the word's usage. For Hebrew words, the first usage of the word in the Scripture, primarily if used in the Torah, is essential. For the Greek words, the Christian Scriptures are used to determine the word usage in the Scripture. Sometimes finding the equivalent Greek word in the Septuagint then analyzing its usage in Hebrew can be very helpful.

The Rules of Hillel are used when applicable. Hillel was a Torah scholar who lived shortly before Jesus's day. Hillel developed several rules for Torah students to interpret the Scriptures which refer to halachic Midrash. In several cases, these rules are helpful in the analysis of the Scripture.

The cultural implications from the period of the writing are done after the linguistic analysis is completed. The culture is crucial because it is not explicitly referenced in the biblical narratives, as indicated earlier.

From the linguistic analysis and the cultural understanding, it is possible to obtain a deeper meaning of the Scripture beyond the literal meaning of the plain text. That is what the listeners of Jesus's time were doing. They put the linguistics and culture together without even having to contemplate it. They simply did it.

The analysis will lead to a set of findings explaining what the passage meant in Jesus's day. Most of the time, the Hebraic analysis leads to the desire for more in-depth analysis to fully understand what Jesus was talking about or what was happening to Him. Whatever the result, a new, more in-depth understanding of the Scripture is obtained.

The components of the Process of Discovery are:

Language

  Process of Discovery

    Linguistics Section

      Linguistic Structure

      Discussion

Questioning the Passage

Verse Comparison of citations or proof text

Translation Inconsistencies

Biblical Personalities

Biblical Locations

Phrase Study

Scripture cross-references

Linguistic Echoes

Rules of Hillel

Culture Section

Discussion

Questioning the passage

Cultural Echoes

Culture and Linguistics Section

Discussion

Midrash

Zohar

Thoughts

Reflections

Only the application sections are included in this document.

Matthew 16:21-23

New American Standard 1995	Koine Greek
21 From that time Jesus began to show His disciples that He must go to Jerusalem, and suffer many things from the elders and chief priests and scribes, and be killed, and be raised up on the third day. 22 Peter took Him aside and began to rebuke Him, saying, "God forbid *it*, Lord! This shall never happen to You." 23 But He turned and said to Peter, "Get behind Me, Satan! You are a stumbling	21 Ἀπὸ τότε ἤρξατο ὁ Ἰησοῦς δεικνύειν τοῖς μαθηταῖς αὐτοῦ ὅτι δεῖ αὐτὸν ἀπελθεῖν εἰς Ἱεροσόλυμα, καὶ πολλὰ παθεῖν ἀπὸ τῶν πρεσβυτέρων καὶ ἀρχιερέων καὶ γραμματέων, καὶ ἀποκτανθῆναι, καὶ τῇ τρίτῃ ἡμέρᾳ ἐγερθῆναι. 22 Καὶ προσλαβόμενος αὐτὸν ὁ Πέτρος ἤρξατο ἐπιτιμᾶν αὐτῷ λέγων, Ἵλεώς σοι, κύριε· οὐ μὴ ἔσται σοι τοῦτο. 23 Ὁ δὲ στραφεὶς εἶπεν τῷ Πέτρῳ, Ὕπαγε ὀπίσω μου, Σατανᾶ, σκάνδαλόν μου εἶ· ὅτι οὐ

block to Me; for you are not setting your mind on God's interests, but man's."	φρονεῖς τὰ τοῦ θεοῦ, ἀλλὰ τὰ τῶν ἀνθρώπων.

Process of Discovery

Linguistics Section

Linguistic Structure

A [Jesus spoke] [21] From that time Jesus began to show His disciples that He must go to Jerusalem, and suffer many things from the elders and chief priests and scribes, and be killed, and be raised up on the third day.

> **B [Peter spoke]** [22] Peter took Him aside and began to rebuke Him, saying, "God forbid *it*, Lord! This shall never happen to You."

A'[Jesus spoke] [23] But He turned and said to Peter, "Get behind Me, Satan! You are a stumbling block to Me; for you are not setting your mind on God's interests, but man's."

Discussion

This short narrative creates a chiasm based on who spoke.

Questioning the Passage[4]

1. Where were Jesus and the disciples? (general question)

   According to the flow of the text, they are still at Ceasera Philippi overlooking the Grotto of Pan. The mistranslation of the word שָׂטָן ,

   which is explained in detail in the Cultural Section, and the scene being at the Grotto of Pan led to the incorrect translation of Jesus's Aramaic words into Greek. The risk of mistranslation always exists between languages.

---

[4] (The questions and answers offered are for discussion purposes. You may have different questions and answers. Remember all questions are valid and all answers must be defendable from Scripture. This applies to this section and to the Culture Section.)

2. Why did Jesus talk about His death? (general question)

There is a scholarly belief that the early Christian communities needed to create precise stories that Jesus told His disciples about His life and death. It was well known from history that prophets die in Jerusalem. Kings and princes did not like being told that they were violating the Laws of the LORD. The prophets of old were commissioned by the LORD to bring the words of repentance to Kings and princes. The usual response from the authority figures was to put the prophetic messenger to death. The King and princes might acknowledge that their actions were against the word of the LORD, but few wanted to be told what they had to do.

Jesus was no different. During His life, He learned what happened to John the Baptist. John told Herod Antipas that marrying his brother's wife was against the Laws of the LORD. Instead of repenting, Herod had John killed for speaking out against the King. The idea of killing off the LORD's prophet was still in play in Jesus's day.

Jesus went to Jerusalem to tell the religious leaders that the LORD was not pleased with them. History says that Jesus was going to suffer and die because of the message that He needed to bring because He would have been viewed as a prophet.

3. What did Jesus mean about Peter's interest and not that of the LORD's? (v. 23)

Jesus believed that Peter's words were instigated by Peter's desires not to lose his best friend, mentor, and religious leader. Peter received the divine revelation that Jesus was the Messiah, and in the next verse, he is told that his Messiah had to die to fulfill the LORD's plan. Acknowledging the LORD's plan was very difficult for Peter to handle. Peter's reaction was a natural human reaction, and that was to save his friend. Jesus had to tell Peter that it was the LORD's plan that had to be implemented. The human plan that came into Peter's mind was not the answer.

Culture Section

Discussion

Jesus's disciples believed that when the Messiah arrived that all the Gentile and pagan kingdoms would bow down to the Davidic Kingdom. The new Hebraic Kingdom would conquer all the Gentile kingdoms and end the threat of annihilation that existed since Abraham walked the Earth. Besides, the Isaiah prophecy about the suffering Messiah was unknown to them. So when Jesus spoke of His suffering and death at the hands of the religious leadership in Jerusalem, the disciples became concerned and alarmed. Peter did not understand that Jesus had to suffer a humiliating death so that the gates of

Heaven would be opened to the LORD's people.[5]

Jesus taught His disciples about the Kingdom of Heaven, not the Davidic Kingdom. Jesus was probably surprised at Peter's response, and that drew some anger. In His anger, Jesus said to Peter, get behind Him, and called him Satan. However, Satan, as we call the personification of evil today, had a different name in Jesus's day which is found in Matthew's Gospel. That name is Beelzebul. This name can be found in Matthew 10:25, 12:24, and 12:27. The question is if Jesus were calling Peter Satan, even in anger, He would have used the word Beelzebul.

---

[5] Rocco A. Errico and George M. Lamsa, *Aramaic Light on the Gospel of Matthew: a Commentary on the Teachings of Jesus from the Aramaic and Unchanged Near Eastern Customs* (Santa Fe, NM: Noohra Foundation, 2000).

The name Satan which is derived from the Hebrew word שָׂטָן has become almost universal in languages around the world to mean the personification of evil, the Devil, Satan. However, in its original Hebraic שָׂטָן and Aramaic, it has a different meaning. Since Jesus would have been speaking Aramaic when talking to His disciples, then the examination of satan in its Aramaic form is necessary. The word *satan* is derived from the root word *sata*. *Sata* means "to mislead, miss the mark, slip, slide, or to deviate from one's course."[6]

From Jesus's point of view, Peter was trying to mislead and deviate Jesus from the divine course

---

[6] IBID.

that He had to follow. Jesus was making it clear that Peter and the other disciples did not understand the real purpose of the Messiah and that the traditional view of the Messiah was not the path of the Messiah. They were not aware of the Suffering Servant prophecy of the Messiah. Indeed they did not want the Messiah to be killed because of their understanding of the Messiah. The disciples expected Jesus to rid them of the Roman oppressors. Jesus must have thought that He communicated the true path of the Messiah as the Suffering Servant and was surprised that Peter did not understand it. Jesus said to Peter to get out of His way and not to try to deviate Jesus from the divine path.

JESUS DID NOT CALL PETER SATAN!

The disciples did not know the Suffering Servant path of the Messiah. The incorrect understanding of the Hebrew word שָׂטָן , which is the same word in Aramaic is where the current church interpretation of what Jesus said to Peter originated. As was said earlier, if Jesus wanted to call Peter Satan, He would have said: "Get behind me Beelzebub!"

The problem with the mistranslation of שָׂטָן starts with the Koine Greek. The translation used in the Greek is Σατανᾶ. From the Koine Greek, the name Satan spread out to the translations of Matthew's Gospel. The English translation in the King James version is Satan. From that point on, English translations of Matthew's Gospel say, "Get behind me, Satan."

Church tradition is dominant with Bible publishers. Publishers are in business to make money and not necessarily to offer the proper translations. Since church tradition out trumps the actual biblical text in so many areas of Christianity it is not surprising that it is done here.

Until the church is ready to return to the original meaning of Matthew's Gospel, this mistranslation and others like it will continue to be made.

Thoughts

Peter thought that he knew what the LORD's plan
was for the restoration of Israel. When Jesus said
that he was going to die at the hands of the
Hebraic leadership, Peter was compelled to say
"not going to happen." How many people today
believe that they know what the LORD's plan is?
Many Christians say that they know that they are
going to Heaven. How do they know that? In the
case of Peter he believed that he knew the
LORD's plan for the Messiah. It turned out that
he did not. So, how does one discover the true
plan the LORD has for their life? That is a part of
the discernment that is necessary to discover the
plan. In ancient days prayer was the way to
discover the plan. Prayer was a time to be quiet
and listen for the voice of the LORD telling His
people what He wanted to be done. Today people

offer their words of prayer and rarely sit back and listen for the LORD. Listening to the LORD takes time and patience. The needed patience to wait for the LORD's answer is not an integral part of society today.

Reflections

The idea of the stumbling block is in several places in the Christian Scriptures. Sometimes a stumbling block is created when a person believes that they have the only meaning of the Scripture. Each denomination of the church preaches that it has the only and correct interpretation of the Scripture. What is seen in this short narrative is that the church can have an incorrect interpretation? The mistranslation of the Hebrew and Aramaic word *satan* as the personification of evil, Satan, had made followers of Jesus believe that he called Peter Satan when He did not. What this shows is that the church has locked the interpretation of Scripture and for centuries anyone who challenged the church interpretation was called heretics and put to death in many different ways. The idea of questioning the

Scripture for a deeper understanding is not allowed. Those days are coming to an end. How could Jesus call His number one disciple Satan? Well the church said so. The prevailing belief for 2000 years is that church must be right. In this case the church is incorrect. However, many Christians may read the case presented that Jesus did not call Peter Satan and will reject it before even reading it. Why? The church has learned over its 2000 years how to enforce its beliefs on Christians. Today Christians should arise and question everything that the church, no matter the denomination, says to be truth. Searching and discovering the original meaning of Scripture is paramount today so that the questions of the younger generation can be answered.

Jesus DID NOT call Peter Satan!

Works Cited

1986. *Back to School.* Directed by James Signorelli. Performed by Rodney Dangerfield.

Davis, Anne Kimball. 2012. *The Synoptic Gospels.* Albuquerque.

Errico, Rocco A., and George M. Lamsa. 2000. *Aramaic Light on the Gospel of Matthew.* Santa Fe, NM: Noohra Foundation.

Made in the USA
Monee, IL
16 April 2022